FINDING FREEDOM IN JESUS

PRESENTED TO

BY

DATE

Lifeway Press®
Brentwood, Tennessee

ISBN 978-1-4300-9522-4
Item 005847588
Dewey Decimal Classification Number: 242
Subject Heading: DEVOTIONAL LITERATURE / BIBLE STUDY AND TEACHING / GOD

Printed in the United States of America.

Student Ministry Publishing
Lifeway Resources
200 Powell Place, Suite 100
Brentwood, Tennessee 37027

We believe that the Bible has God for its author; salvation for its end; truth, without any mixture of error, for its matter; and that all Scripture is totally true and trustworthy. To review Lifeway's doctrinal guideline, please visit https://www.lifeway.com/about/doctrinal-guidelines.

---

publishing team

Director, Next Gen Ministries
Chuck Peters

Manager, Small Group Resources
Karen Daniel

Writer
Mary Margaret West

Content Editor
Kyle Wiltshire

Production Editor
April-Lyn Caouette

Cover Designer
Lauren Ervin

Graphic Designer
Lisa Olian

TABLE OF CONTENTS

INTRO

The idea of being set free sounds amazing, right? It sounds like no rules, no boundaries, and endless opportunity. But that's not the kind of freedom we're talking about. As we look at the Bible over the next thirty days, you'll see that there's a difference between being set free and actually living out that freedom. God's desire is for you to walk in freedom. We see this all through the New Testament. Jesus came to set you free so that you would do something with that freedom—and so others can see Him in you!

We're going to look at Bible verses that will help and encourage you along the way. You aren't alone in this, and there's so much you can learn if you're ready and willing. As you move toward living set free, Jesus will change your life in ways you never expected. We'll see that He wants us to love our enemies, be full of hope, live in truth, and be confident in all that He has for us. He is good and can be trusted!

My prayer for you is that you would take on this challenge of changing some things in your life and let God do the work inside of you. If you have a relationship with Jesus, you've already been set free! It's the best feeling in the world. You have total access to God, and the Holy Spirit lives in you as your guide. Now your call is to live in the freedom God gives. Living like Jesus isn't easy or for the faint of heart, but it's absolutely worth it.

GETTING STARTED

This devotional contains thirty days of content, broken down into sections. Each day is divided into three elements—**discover**, **delight**, and **display**—to help you grow in your relationship with God.

DISCOVER

This section helps you examine the Bible in light of who God is and determine what it says about your identity in relationship to Him. Included here is the daily Bible reading and key verses, along with illustrations and commentary to guide you as you learn more about God's Word.

DELIGHT

In this section, you'll be challenged by questions and activities that help you see how God is alive and active in every detail of His Word and your life.

DISPLAY

Here's where you take action. This section calls you to apply what you've learned through each day.

Each day also includes a prayer activity at the conclusion of the devotion.

Throughout the devotional, you'll also find extra items to help you connect with the topic of the book personally, such as Scripture memory verses and interactive articles.

SECTION 1

SET FREE FROM...

Knowing Jesus sets you free from who you used to be. He lifts your head and sets you free from shame, loneliness, hopelessness, and fear so you can live out your faith. As you fix your eyes on Him, you'll see freedom begin to take over every part of your life.

DAY 1

LIVING SET FREE

READ ROMANS 6:15-23.

But now, since you have been set free from sin and
have become enslaved to God, you have your fruit,
which results in sanctification—and the outcome is eternal life!
— Romans 6:22

DISCOVER

Have you ever wanted more freedom? Maybe you've asked your parents for more freedom or you just wish you had more ability to go where you want to go and do what you want to do. This isn't quite what freedom in Christ is. It isn't the ability to do whatever you want—it's the freedom you have when you know Him as your Savior and live in a way that honors Him. He has set you free from sin so that you can honor Him with your life!

In Romans 6, it's clear that sin is the thing that holds us back from truly knowing Jesus. Every day we find ourselves wrestling with sin, and Jesus is the only one who can rescue us. Romans 6:23 tells us exactly this—and the payment for our sin is Jesus's death. Jesus entered the picture and took on our sin so we can be forgiven. Amazing!

Over the next thirty days, we'll explore what it means to live set free. Romans 6:22 gives us this outline of what it looks like when we are set free by Jesus: Being enslaved to God means you belong to Him. This is the best thing that could ever happen to you! He makes you His for all of eternity. Once you are His, the Spirit gives you gifts that bear fruit in your life and point other people to Jesus (see Gal. 5:22-23). *Sanctification* is a big word for the lifelong process of becoming more and more like Jesus. You won't ever become totally sanctified until you meet Jesus face to face in heaven for all of eternity. That is what it looks like to be set free!

DELIGHT

What's the difference between being set free and living set free?

What is a part of living set free that feels confusing or difficult to you?

What is holding you back from living a life set free in Jesus?

DISPLAY

Freedom should make us feel truly set free, not bound or held captive by anything or anyone. God's freedom for us is unlike any other kind of freedom you'll ever experience. It's not just life changing—it's eternity changing! Whether or not you know Jesus, you're in the right place. Be committed to keep spending time in God's Word and getting to know Him by completing this book. True freedom is found only in Him, my friend!

God, thank You for the gift of freedom You give to us. Let us live like we're free and let others see that freedom in our daily lives.

DAY 2

SHAMELESS

READ 1 PETER 2:1-10.

For it stands in Scripture: See, I lay a stone in Zion, a chosen and honored cornerstone, and the one who believes in him will never be put to shame.
— 1 Peter 2:6

DISCOVER

Have you ever felt ashamed? Sometimes we bring shame on ourselves, and other times someone else makes us feel ashamed. Shame often makes us want to hide from our circumstances. But when you live a life that's set free in Jesus, He takes your shame and gives you a new perspective and outlook. When you know Him, He lifts your head when you are clothed in shame (see Ps. 3:3).

In today's key verse, Peter is actually quoting the book of Isaiah in the Old Testament (see Isa. 28:16). God declared that those who believe in Him wouldn't live in shame. God's perspective is so different than ours, and some of the people who the world would reject are exactly the ones whom God chooses to use.

Jesus wants you to live without shame. You can't go back and undo things that have already happened, but Jesus has given you a new hope and a new outlook. He takes your shame and gets rid of it—and He gets all the glory! He's changing each of us who know Him from the inside out. He does this so that we can point others to Him. The world doesn't understand how shame could be lifted because they don't think it should be. Only through a relationship with Jesus can we find a life where our shame has been taken away by someone else.

DELIGHT

What's something that can cause shame in a person's life?

What do you think Peter means in 1 Peter 2:9 when he lists who we are as believers and then says that Jesus has "called you out of darkness into his marvelous light"?

Are you living in darkness or in light? How do you know?

DISPLAY

If you had to rank yourself on a scale of 1–10 (where 1 is living in shame and 10 is living in total freedom), where would you put yourself? What's one next step you can take to move closer towards freedom? If you've been living in shame, today is a great day to ask God to show you how to live in freedom through Him. His desire is that you wouldn't live in shame but that you would look to Him instead.

God, be the lifter of my head today. Let any shame I'm holding on to be gone and help me to live in freedom. Help me to fix my eyes on You so that I can leave shame behind and never look back.

DAY 3

RESCUE PLAN

READ COLOSSIANS 1:9-14

He has rescued us from the domain of darkness and transferred us into the kingdom of the Son he loves.
— Colossians 1:13

DISCOVER

One of the craziest things about living set free is that sometimes we convince ourselves that we aren't actually free. Satan will do everything he can to make us think we still have to live in shame and darkness, when the reality is that Jesus came to do free us from that. Jesus's death, burial, and resurrection are the hinge of His great rescue plan for us. Because of what Jesus did, we get to turn the page and live like we've been rescued from darkness. Why? Because we have! It's not a joke—it's truth.

Paul, the author of the book of Colossians, clearly says that he's praying for the believers to know this down deep in their bones. He's praying that they would be filled with knowledge, truth, and power to overcome Satan's plans to keep them distracted and living in shame. He encourages believers to "walk worthy of the Lord"; that's for every single one of us. We have been rescued! The Lord's plans for us are good, and He has done everything He can do to make sure we know that wholeheartedly.

What we have to know is that none of this happens on accident. We must do our part to grow in Christ and know Him more on a daily basis. You're doing that by spending time in God's Word right here! It's a lifelong process of growing closer to Him and having a better understanding of His good plan for you. He came to rescue you, my friend!

DELIGHT

What does it mean to "walk worthy of the Lord"?

How can you "give thanks to the Father" for what He has done for you?

Are you living like you've been rescued? Why or why not?

DISPLAY

As you prioritize your relationship with God, the goal is for you to grow closer to Him and live more and more set free. We will always be humans, and we won't ever be able to completely live set free until we get to heaven. However, our job is to do our best to honor God on a daily basis as we live and grow. What is one way you can honor God today and grow closer to Him?

God, I give You my life. Let me live set free and in a good, healthy relationship with You. I want to honor You with everything, so help me see ways I can grow and become more like You.

DAY 4

UNASHAMED

READ ROMANS 8:1-11.

Therefore, there is now no condemnation for those in Christ Jesus, because the law of the Spirit of life in Christ Jesus has set you free from the law of sin and death.
— Romans 8:1-2

DISCOVER

Are you starting to sense a theme here? The Bible talks A LOT about being set free, so we should definitely pay attention.

If you don't know it yet, eternity is a super long time. It's literally forever. Make sense? No matter how we try to explain it, we can't fully wrap our minds around it. Our lives are so short in comparison to eternity.

Because of our sin, the harsh reality is that we deserve death and separation from God. BUT JESUS. Jesus entered the picture, died on the cross for our sins, and created a way for us to have eternal life with Him. He has set us free so that we can live in freedom on a daily basis!

Has someone ever condemned or judged you for something you've done? If this hasn't happened yet, it will. Today's verses open by saying, "There is now no condemnation for those in Christ Jesus." This is a huge deal. If you know Jesus, God doesn't see your sin when He looks at you; He only sees someone who is set free. If you are in Christ Jesus, live like it! Being set free isn't a permission slip to do whatever you want. It means you are called to make your life line up with who Jesus is and what He has done for you. That's where true freedom lies.

DELIGHT

What does it mean to condemn something or someone?

Think of someone who has hurt you. How hard would it be to completely forget everything he or she has done to hurt you? Why?

Do you think it's hard for Jesus to look at you after what you've done that has hurt Him? Why or why not?

DISPLAY

If you've ever felt shamed by someone, you know it's not fun. As brothers and sisters in Christ, we need to live the way Jesus lived and not put shame and condemnation on others. We are not the Holy Spirit. It's not our job to try to make others feel badly for what they've done. This doesn't mean we ignore sin and say it's okay. It means we live willing to forgive as we've been forgiven. What would it look like if you were a person who didn't put shame on others but pointed them to Jesus? It's so different than what we see in the world around us, but it's what we are called to do. There's no condemnation on you, so don't condemn or shame others. Let them see Jesus in you!

God, help us to live in freedom and realize that because of Jesus, we are no longer condemned. Help us to point others to Him in the way we live our lives and the way we respond to things that happen to us and around us. Let my relationship with You bring glory to Your name in every circumstance.

DAY 5

I HATE YOU, BUT I LOVE YOU

READ 1 JOHN 3:13-18.

We know that we have passed from death to life because we love our brothers and sisters. The one who does not love remains in death.
— 1 John 3:14

DISCOVER

Does the idea of someone hating you make you cringe? For most of us, the idea is straight up painful. Today's verses basically say that because of Jesus, the world is going to hate you, and you shouldn't be surprised when it happens. Ugh. If you're a people pleaser, this is like a worst case scenario.

What it really boils down to is this: It's not you that they hate, it's Jesus. As you walk in relationship with Him, you begin to act and look more and more like Him. It shows in the way you talk, the way you treat people, and the way you respond in difficult situations, because you're no longer the same person. Christ in you makes all the difference in the world!

The Bible gives many examples of how we are to love those who hate us, persecute us, speak out against us, or treat us badly. Just like we've talked about the last few days, living set free doesn't mean life is going to be easy. Jesus was hated by many people, but it was because they didn't understand who He was. As you live like Him, people won't understand how you have the peace, freedom, and joy that loving Jesus brings into your life. They won't understand how you keep loving people, even when they hate you, or how you continue to be kind and compassionate, even when it hurts. There will likely still be circumstances when you will need to walk away from a situation that's unhealthy or harmful—and when this happens, make sure you find a trusted adult you can talk to. But loving Jesus means you won't always be liked or appreciated by others.

DELIGHT

In the past, how have you responded when someone was unkind or hateful towards you?

What are some circumstances where you need to walk away from a hurtful person or situation? Who is a trustworthy adult you could talk to when this happens?

What does it mean to "let us not love in word or speech, but in action and in truth" (1 John 3:18)?

DISPLAY

Walking with Jesus brings both joy and heartache, but He is worth it! Keep your eyes fixed on Him, no matter what. Our actions speak louder than our words, and loving those who hate us (although who they really hate is Jesus in us) can make a profound difference in the lives of those around us. While we shouldn't let people walk all over us, be kind and compassionate as you treat others the way Jesus would. What is one way you can love others even when they are hateful toward you because of your faith in Jesus?

Lord, when life gets hard, remind me that I'm not alone. Jesus suffered, and I don't want to be surprised when it happens to me. Let my love for You be so strong that everyone around me can see it, and let me honor You in the way I treat the people You place in my path.

DAY 6

A REASON TO GO

READ MATTHEW 28:16-20.

"Go, therefore, and make disciples of all nations, baptizing them in the name of the Father and of the Son and of the Holy Spirit . . ."
— Matthew 28:19

DISCOVER

The Bible verses for today are the last words Matthew recorded Jesus speaking to His disciples before He ascended back into heaven. If I knew I was about to speak my last words, I would make sure they were intentional and purposeful. It would be crazy for us to overlook these verses because Jesus was intentional with what He said. He gives a clear directive: "Go." Why is this so significant? Because we have work to do here on earth throughout our lives! Jesus gives three clear directives:

1. Make disciples.
2. Baptize them.
3. Teach them.

Through church, mission work, and other discipleship methods, we are called to make this happen. Who are you learning about Jesus from? Those are the people who have discipled you. Have you been baptized since you started a relationship with Jesus? If not, talk to an adult who loves Jesus about taking that step of obedience. As you grow in Christ, teach others what you're learning. You don't have to know everything to tell other people about Jesus—you just have to be willing to share. It's not as complicated as it may sound, I promise!

Jesus is clear that we have work to do, and we don't want to miss out. Doing His work is part of being set free.

DELIGHT

If you knew you had to say your last words and make them count, who would you say them to and what would you say?

What's your role in fulfilling the Great Commission (see Matt. 28:18-20)?

DISPLAY

As your life looks more and more like Jesus's, don't put your work for Him ahead of your own relationship with Him. Spend time with Him daily (like you're doing right now) and let that be the priority in your life before you minister to others. You need to serve others out of what God is teaching you, and you have to spend time with Him to learn and grow! What is one thing you have learned so far through this devotional book? How can you pass it along to someone else?

God, help me to live out the Great Commission in a way that honors You and brings You glory. I want to live my life saying yes when You tell me to go and follow You. Let my words and actions show that this is who I am and that I love You with my whole heart.

MEMORY VERSES

THEREFORE, THERE IS NOW NO CONDEMNATION FOR THOSE IN CHRIST JESUS, BECAUSE THE LAW OF THE SPIRIT OF LIFE IN CHRIST JESUS HAS SET YOU FREE FROM THE LAW OF SIN AND DEATH.

ROMANS 8:1-2

DAY 7

DISCIPLESHIP

READ MATTHEW 28:16-20.

". . . teaching them to observe everything I have commanded you. And remember, I am with you always, to the end of the age."
— Matthew 28:20

DISCOVER

We're taking another look at the last words of Jesus in Matthew, but digging into a different key verse today. Jesus tells His disciples that even though He's not going to be with them on earth anymore, He will still always be with them. This is possible through the Holy Spirit. He also teaches His followers to obey everything He commanded them.

Jesus spent three years pouring everything into the lives of His disciples. He led by example, performed miracles, raised the dead, confronted bullies, showed compassion . . . and the list goes on. Jesus's goal was to teach His disciples everything so that they could live the same way and tell others about what they had seen and heard. They knew Jesus, and what He invested in them lived on in each of their lives.

This is what we call *discipleship*. Discipleship is learning from someone else and following that person's lead, which points to Jesus. As a Christian, it's how we grow and learn. Jesus set an example for His disciples to learn from, and we must follow His lead. You're not too young to help someone else learn about Jesus. When I was in high school, a girl a few grades ahead of me met with me and a couple of my friends before school one day a week. We learned about the Bible together and prayed for each other. It doesn't have to be complicated, and you don't have to have all of the answers. Just be willing to help others to live set free and follow where Jesus leads.

DELIGHT

If you could have one person with you always, who would it be and why?

What adult in your life is pointing you towards Jesus? Why do you want to follow that adult's lead?

If you don't yet have someone discipling you, who is someone you want to learn from and why?

DISPLAY

Pray that God would send someone to disciple you. If you've been walking with Jesus for a while, pray that He would also send someone who you can disciple. What would it look like if you took what you knew and shared it? Think about all you could learn from someone who has been walking with Jesus longer than you have. No matter what happens, Jesus will be with you always!

Jesus, thank You for the example You set. Remind me that You are always with me, and show me who else I can learn from and lead so we can grow in You together. Help me to remember these important words that You gave the disciples so I don't get discouraged. Thank You for being with me!

DAY 8

WHO, ME?

READ GALATIANS 6:1-5.

Carry one another's burdens; in this way you will fulfill the law of Christ.
— Galatians 6:2

DISCOVER

Have you ever prayed for someone you don't know? Maybe you saw a social media post, a friend asked you to pray, or you saw a situation that you know you needed to pray about. We get to be part of something much bigger than ourselves when we come together as Christians. Today's verses say, "Carry one another's burdens," and this is exactly what it means! We unite over things that matter because we have Jesus in common.

One of the best things about being a Christian is that you're never alone. Jesus is always with you, and you also are a part of a family of believers around the world! There's something crazy that happens: The common bond we have in Jesus ties us together in a way that's hard to explain.

The rest of today's verses are a reminder that we have to stay humble. Every person is one step away from a big mistake, but it's easy to think, "It could never happen to ____." That blank could have your name in it or it could be the name of someone else you really respect. We need to be people who encourage others to do the right, God-honoring thing. Be on guard so that you don't get tangled up in someone else's sin and end up sinning yourself. When God looks at you, you aren't judged by anyone else's mistakes or sins—just your own. You are responsible for yourself, but you still need to come alongside other believers and help carry their burdens as much as you can.

DELIGHT

What is a situation you know of right now where you can help bear someone else's burden by praying? Stop right now and pray for this person or situation.

Why is it important for Christians to bear one another's burdens?

When was a time you were tempted to sin because of someone else's bad choices? Why was it hard to say yes or no in that situation?

DISPLAY

How do you stay humble? It's easier said than done, right? It's not about you getting the glory. What's a situation in your world right now where you can help carry someone else's burden but not ask for the credit? How can you come alongside someone in your life, make his or her load lighter, and trust that God sees and knows? Take action and don't miss an opportunity to serve the Lord by serving someone else.

God, help me to remember that it's not about me—it's about Your glory. Give me eyes to see people around me who need my prayers and actions, and remind me that it's all about You.

DAY 9

DEALING HOPE

READ ROMANS 5:1-5.

This hope will not disappoint us, because God's love has been poured out in our hearts through the Holy Spirit who was given to us.
— Romans 5:5

DISCOVER

Do you like card games? Most of them require someone to be the dealer, the person who shuffles and passes out the cards. These verses in Romans are talking about a dealer, but not a dealer of cards—a dealer of hope. Jesus is the ultimate dealer of hope. He has endless amounts of hope to share, and He's in the business of being generous.

If you know Jesus, there is never a moment in life where you're without hope. Jesus gives us a hope that can't be taken away, and we get to see it played out in our lives through the Holy Spirit. Not only does He deal out hope, but as these verses also tell us, "This hope will not disappoint us," because what Jesus has to offer is just that good.

It's when we lose sight of Jesus that we lose sight of hope. He doesn't move—we are the ones who take our eyes off Him because of distractions in the world or in our lives. Jesus truly sets us free from hopelessness because God's love has been poured into our hearts through the Holy Spirit. We can't get away from Him, no matter how hard we try. He loves us so much that He forgives us and pours out His love in such huge ways. Don't miss it!

DELIGHT

What gives you hope?

What makes you feel hopeless?

How have you experienced the hope Jesus offers?

DISPLAY

Think of a situation in your life or in the world around you that feels hopeless. How can Jesus make a difference in that particular circumstance? How could it change things if Jesus showed up in the middle of it? Ask God to show you ways to deal hope into that situation.

Jesus, You are good. Thank You for the amazing hope You give me. Help me to be a hope dealer like You are; help me to bring hope into the lives of people around me. Thank You for always bringing hope into every situation.

DAY 10

FINAL WORD

READ HEBREWS 2:14-18.

Now since the children have flesh and blood in common, Jesus also shared in these, so that through his death he might destroy the one holding the power of death—that is, the devil—and free those who were held in slavery all their lives by the fear of death.
— Hebrews 2:14-15

DISCOVER

Death is hard. Here on earth, we feel the pain, sorrow, and grief that comes with death, and there's no way around it. As a believer, death is still a painful reality, but it's not without hope. Jesus conquered Satan and provided life for each of us, and this sets us free—not from physical death itself, but from the fear of death. We don't have to be afraid of death as Christians because our hope is in Jesus. Jesus's death on the cross for our sins gives us eternal life, so death doesn't get the last word—Jesus does.

We still grieve because of death, but we also rejoice because our eternity is secure through Jesus. It will still be hard, but our hope lets us look beyond the loss to eternity, and that's where we fix our eyes. Have you ever thought about what it must be like to finish your race here on earth and arrive in heaven to a peace, joy, and hope that we can't even imagine on earth? There's no sorrow or tears there. In 2 Corinthians 5:8, Paul says, "We would prefer to be away from the body and at home with the Lord." Jesus is our hope and our home. We won't be longing for life here on earth because we will be in the presence of our Lord and Savior for eternity!

Let me remind you: We have a responsibility to tell the people around us about Jesus. It's worth the risk because the cost is eternity. Death will not have the final word for Christians. We are set free from the fear of death because of the hope we have in Jesus.

DELIGHT

Who do you know who needs the hope of Jesus? Pray for this individual right now. Use the space below to write your prayer.

Jesus gives us hope even in death. How does that change the way you view death?

DISPLAY

What if one of your friends hears about Jesus in his or her twenties or thirties and realizes that even though you knew about Jesus, you didn't bother to share about Him? What would that tell your friend about your love for Jesus? What would that say about your love for your friend?

Friend, what do you have to lose? Don't miss the opportunities that God gives you to tell the people in your life about Him.

God, give me the courage to tell others about You. When I don't know what to say, give me the words and help me to be a light for You wherever I go. Thank You for giving us hope even in death.

SECTION 2

SET FREE TO...

You have been set free to live like Jesus! As you walk with Jesus, He gives you the confidence and wisdom to let this freedom change your life. Walking in obedience to Him gives you more freedom than you could ever imagine.

DAY 11

THE UPSIDE DOWN

READ MATTHEW 5:43-48.

"You have heard that it was said, Love your neighbor and hate your enemy." — Matthew 5:43

DISCOVER

Jesus's ways are upside down, and these verses today show us just that! Love your enemies? Pray for people who make your life hard? That feels like the total opposite of what we should be doing. It boils down to this—this is how we live like Jesus, and living like this is how we are set free. So much of what He did was the opposite of what people expected Him to do. He was a mystery to many He encountered, but everywhere He went, He left a trail of changed lives in His wake.

When you've been hurt by someone, what is your first instinct on how to respond? For most of us, our first instinct isn't to pray for that person—but that's what Jesus tells us to do. It's insanely easy to pray for people who love you well, but is so hard to pray for those who have hurt you or hurt people you love.

There's freedom in living like Jesus and loving others the way He loves. You, my friend, have been set free to love like Jesus. This upside-down way of thinking and living looks crazy to the world, but there's a beautiful freedom in it. Followers of Christ aren't supposed to love and live like the world. Jesus was radical and turned our world upside down, but He did it with compassion, kindness, and genuine authority. What do you have to lose by loving like Jesus?

DELIGHT

Think of a situation where you didn't love your enemies. What could have been different if your approach was like Jesus's?

When have you shown love to someone who wasn't loving you in return? What was the result of living in Jesus's upside-down way?

DISPLAY

Have you ever struggled with people in your family, feeling like they're the enemy? What if today you decided you're going to respond differently than you ever have before? You alone are responsible for yourself, your actions, and your reactions. You can't control anyone else. What if you decided to love instead of react to what they say to you? Put this into practice and pray that God will change your heart and the hearts of those you struggle with.

God, change me from the inside out. Let my life be upside down like Jesus's. Please give me what I need to be bold and show love and kindness, even when it's hard. Keep my eyes fixed on You when I'm attacked. Let me love like You do.

DAY 12

RULE BREAKER

READ ROMANS 7:4-6.

But now we have been released from the law, since we have died to what held us, so that we may serve in the newness of the Spirit and not in the old letter of the law.
— Romans 7:6

DISCOVER

Have you ever seen a sign describing a rule that just seemed absurd? Most of the time, this happens because someone did something so ridiculous that they had to make a new rule about it. Crazy, right? For instance, there was a time when people were foolishly eating laundry detergent pods, so companies had to add a label to their products warning that they're poisonous and not to eat them.

Some of you are rule followers and others are rule breakers. Jesus was both. He followed all of God's instructions but broke the made-up rules that the religious leaders of His day had put into place. He knew that those things weren't from God, so He did what He knew was right.

Your job is to follow Jesus and serve others around you. You don't do it because it's the rules but because it honors God. As a student, you are called to obey your parents and the rules they make for you. They've been put in a place of authority in your life, and your role is to honor them.

Today's verses say that "we have been released from the law"—that means we are free from all the things that we did to try and please God that He didn't need or ask us to do. Many of us get caught up in making our own laws and living in legalism, doing things to look good in the eyes of others. Jesus sets us free from this so that we can live in a set-free way that honors Him simply because we love Him.

DELIGHT

When was the last time you felt like you were been stuck doing things for God because you were"supposed to" rather than because you wanted to? What should it look like to serve Him from a position of love?

How can you honor God with rules in your life?

DISPLAY

What we're talking about today isn't something that just changes in a day—it's a lifelong process of living like Jesus *every* day. In different seasons of your life, you may find yourself living under the law instead of under the grace of Jesus, and He will remind you that things are out of order. What you're called to do today is honor God and the authorities around you while also living set free like Jesus. Easier said than done, but His mercies are new every morning for all of us. What is one way you can live in grace today rather than under the law?

Pray today that God would give you simple ways to live in freedom and in His grace. Ask Him to remind you when you start living under the law so that you can make a change. Pray for patience for yourself and with those around you as you pursue a life that looks like Jesus.

DAY 13

TRUE WORSHIP

READ ROMANS 12:1-2.

Therefore, brothers and sisters, in view of the mercies of God,
I urge you to present your bodies as a living sacrifice,
holy and pleasing to God; this is your true worship.
— Romans 12:1

DISCOVER

What if I told you that worship isn't just about songs? When we look at our verses for today, we see that worship is about something much bigger and deeper. Worship is your life. Who are you honoring and giving your worship to all day long? Paul is writing to the Roman church, saying that everything about their lives is worship and that they need to be living sacrifices to God in worship to Him.

It's so much easier to just enjoy worship at church or listen to worship songs in the car. Giving up everything is much more complicated. God is asking you to lay down your own wants and needs and submit to His will and direction for your life. This is true worship.

Rather than thinking about worship as a burden, think of it this way—you've been set free by Jesus to worship Him. That begins to change things. He is worthy of our total and complete worship with every part of our lives. He wants all of it: all the relationships, texts, ambitions, goals, frustrations, disappointments, stresses, and anything else you can think of. When you set those things free and submit your life to God in worship, that's when you find real, lasting freedom.

DELIGHT

What are some ways you've worshiped God recently?

What are some changes you need to make to truly worship God with everything? List a few of them.

DISPLAY

Hopefully you're starting to see that the idea of living set free affects every area of your life. It's not just a small change—it means turning everything toward Jesus all the time. Friend, I hope that you see that's where freedom truly is. You have been set free by Jesus to live in freedom. What is something that you need to let go of to worship freely?

God, I worship You right now, right where I am. Let everything I say and do today honor You and bring You glory. I give You all of the areas of my life where I've been holding back so that I can truly worship You with everything. Make my life look like one big worship service!

DAY 14

SECRETS

READ MATTHEW 6:1-4.

"But when you give to the poor, don't let your left hand know what your right hand is doing, so that your giving may be in secret. And your Father who sees in secret will reward you."
— Matthew 6:3-4

DISCOVER

Are you good at keeping secrets? Have you ever found yourself tempted to say, "I'm not supposed to say anything about this, but . . ." and told something that was supposed to stay private? If it's important to sometimes keep secrets for our friend, how much more important must it be to keep some things just between us and God?

As you listen for His voice in your life, there will be opportunities for you to do things for God's glory that you won't get any credit for. If you're like me, that sounds painful. I like to get credit for things I've done! But one more way that God asks us to live in this upside-down kind of way is that He asks us to keep some things just between us and Him.

What kind of things could fit in this category? Things like serving someone who needs some help, giving financially to something or someone in a way that you know God is asking you to, or praying for God to do something and letting Him get all the credit when it happens. Much like you've seen in other verses we've read, it's not about us—it's about God's glory. At the end of the day, He sees and knows, and these verses even say, "And your Father who sees in secret will reward you."

We don't do these things for the reward; we have to trust that God knows best. Sometimes our names will be in lights and we will be noticed, thanked, and shown gratitude. But that's not our goal. We must listen for when God is asking us to stay quiet. Keep your eyes fixed on Him, and the glory that He gets will be so much better than any you could get for yourself.

DELIGHT

What is something God might be prompting you to do where you can serve someone else without anyone knowing?

If you like getting the credit for things, how can you surrender that to God and let it honor Him? If you don't struggle as much with this, how can you practice letting God take the credit even more than you do now?

DISPLAY

Ask God to give you something you can do this week that's just between you and Him. Don't tell anyone you're praying about it—just talk to God and give Him the opportunity to show up and show off. It's amazing what happens when we ask God to do something He loves to do. He wants to use us for this!

God, use me this week! Let me see how You're working and show me how I can love people in my life like You would. Help me to honor You with my life and actions and to seek out opportunities to serve You and point others towards You.

DAY 15

SO FANCY

READ MATTHEW 6:5-8.

"Don't be like them, because your Father knows the things you need before you ask him."
— Matthew 6:8

DISCOVER

In today's verses from Matthew 6, we're reading Jesus's teaching on prayer. Prayer may seem easy on the surface, but sometimes we may feel a little lost when it comes to doing it. Jesus tells His listeners to not flaunt their prayers in front of others, which basically means not to say a lot of big words and fancy things just to draw attention to ourselves. We're having a conversation with a friend. It's not about fancy words or sounding smart; it's about pouring our hearts out to Him. God already knows what's on our hearts, but He wants to hear it directly from us.

The amazing thing is that He isn't surprised, caught off guard, or unprepared for anything you bring to Him in prayer. He just loves you so much that He wants that line of communication to stay open between you. Prayer truly is just talking to God. He knows you better than anyone else and is looking for you to just be yourself before Him. Prayer truly has a way of setting you free to be who God created you to be. Your Father in heaven knows you and loves you.

DELIGHT

Think about a time you struggled with how to pray, either recently or in the past. What do today's verses prompt you to do differently?

Where are some good quiet places for you to pray where you can really focus and not be distracted?

When you are called on to pray in public, how can you follow Jesus's teaching in these verses?

DISPLAY

As you pray, consider writing down the things you pray about in a journal or notebook. Include the date so you can look back and see the way God worked through your prayers. Note cards or a notes app on your phone are great ways to keep track of the things that are important to you. If you have a spot at home, in your locker, in your car, or somewhere else, put those prayers up so you can see them and be reminded to pray more often about the things that God has put on your heart. Don't miss the opportunity to see God at work!

God, when I don't have the words to pray, please give them to me. Remind me that You're more interested in my heart and motives than in how fancy and wordy my prayers are. Give me confidence to come before You with everything on my heart.

DAY 16

FORGOTTEN FORGIVENESS

READ MATTHEW 6:9-15.

"And forgive us our debts, as we also have forgiven our debtors."
— Matthew 6:12

DISCOVER

If you know Jesus, you have been completely forgiven. There's no going back. What an amazing truth to realize! Think about some of the things you've been forgiven—the list is long and detailed, but those things are gone in Jesus's eyes. It's not until your eyes are open to how much you've been forgiven that it becomes easier to forgive others.

Most of us rarely have an issue asking for forgiveness, but it can often be hard to give it to others. When we've been hurt and wounded and we don't like the outcome, we just don't want to give them the satisfaction. But this is so opposite of how Jesus looks at forgiveness. He offers it freely and generously, and we love receiving it from Him.

Forgiving others sets you free. Truthfully, forgiveness is so much more about you than the other person. You're the one holding on to grudges and the past. You're the one who won't let it go. The other person may have moved on from the situation, and you're only hurting yourself at this point by hanging on to it.

Forgiveness is a gift, both as the giver and the receiver. The freedom you find in forgiveness is the kind of thing that changes your life. Jesus isn't asking you to just say the words, but to let freedom wash all over you as you do it. Pull an Elsa and "let it go."

DELIGHT

Is there anyone that you haven't forgiven? In light of what we've looked at today, are you at a place where you can forgive that person or those people now? Why or why not?

Why can forgiveness be so hard?

What do you need to be forgiven for? Is there anyone you need to ask forgiveness from?

DISPLAY

Friend, you are free when you forgive. It's a gift that has the power of life or death, and you get to make the decision how you will use it. You're only responsible for yourself. What is God asking you to do? What do today's verses encourage you to do?

God, thank You for forgiving me. Help me to do the same, even when it's difficult. Help me to live in a way that looks like You, starting with how I forgive others. Let my life be an example to those around me so they can see more of You.

MEMORY VERSE

THEREFORE, LET US APPROACH THE THRONE OF GRACE WITH BOLDNESS, SO THAT WE MAY RECEIVE MERCY AND FIND GRACE TO HELP US IN TIME OF NEED.

HEBREWS 4:16

DAY 17

JESUS KNOWS

READ HEBREWS 4:14-16.

Therefore, let us approach the throne of grace with boldness, so that we may receive mercy and find grace to help us in time of need.
— Hebrews 4:16

DISCOVER

Jesus understands you. He was your age once and He knows what it's like to be rejected, hurt, and tempted. Have you ever thought about the fact that Jesus had friends? He was a good friend and never hurt anyone because He never sinned. Wouldn't you want a friend like that?

Sometimes we think Jesus has no idea what we're going through, but He does. Yes, He lived a perfect life and serves as our "great high priest," but He also experienced life as we know it fully. We have full access to the God of the universe because of Jesus. We are free to approach Him with all our needs, knowing that He understands what we need. He's been there and He can relate to what we go through.

The freedom that comes from knowing Jesus is all over the Bible. He loves you so much that He:

- came to earth and faced all those hard things so He could better relate to you;
- died after living a perfect life and took on your sin so you could spend eternity in heaven with Him; and
- rose from the dead and ascended to heaven, where He now sits at the right hand of God the Father, bringing our needs right to Him.

It brings tears to my eyes to think of how good Jesus is and how much He loves YOU, right where you are, no matter what you've done. Don't miss what He wants to do in and through you!

DELIGHT

Why is it important that Jesus can relate to us?

How does it change your perspective of Jesus to know what He has done for you?

What do you think it means that Jesus is our great High Priest?

DISPLAY

What should change in your life now that you realize in a deeper way how much Jesus loves you and what He has set you free from? What are some practical things you can do today or this week to let it show in your life? Pray that God would give you eyes to see people in your life who don't yet know Jesus. In the space below, write down the names of anyone who came to mind so you can pray for them.

Jesus, You are so much better than I ever imagined. Thank You for loving me enough to do everything You could do to relate to me right where I am. Help me to live my life in a way that shows how much I love You.

DAY 18

TRAINS, PLANES, AND THE GOSPEL

READ ACTS 1:4-8.

"But you will receive power when the Holy Spirit has come on you, and you will be my witnesses in Jerusalem, in all Judea and Samaria, and to the ends of the earth."
— Acts 1:8

DISCOVER

What's the farthest you've ever been from home? Think about how long it took you to get there and what method of travel you used. Maybe you took a train or a road trip, and you saw the landscape change right before your eyes. If you were on a plane, hopefully you were able to see from above and watch the terrain or water far below you.

Today's verses are instructions from Jesus about what the disciples were supposed to do after He ascended back into heaven. He's telling them to go to their hometown, their city, state, country, and world to spread the good news of what He has done.

God may be calling you to go to the farthest, darkest parts of the earth to make sure that everyone knows who Jesus is. Whether or not God sends you around the world, there's no question that He is calling you to your street, your classroom, your workplace, your family, and your friends. We are set here on earth to be witnesses for Jesus wherever we go. The calling on each of our lives looks different, so don't waste time and energy comparing your calling and story to anyone else's. The thing that matters most is this: Are you obedient?

As you go throughout your life, God is giving you the opportunity to take the gospel with you everywhere you go. Don't miss out! Living on mission gives life-changing and life-giving experiences. He longs for us to be engaged in His work and set free to be His witnesses, both at home and to the ends of the earth.

DELIGHT

Where has God currently called you to share the gospel?

What does obedience look like for you right now?

DISPLAY

Have you asked God where He wants you to be a witness? Sometimes we try to do God's work without asking Him for directions, so don't miss out on what He could be preparing you for. God doesn't make mistakes, and He doesn't waste anything. Pray that He will show you where He wants to use you for His glory!

God, use me wherever You want to so that everyone can hear about Jesus. Let them see Your love in both my actions and in my words, not just one or the other. Thank You for giving me opportunities to serve You.

DAY 19

LITTLE WHITE LIES

READ JOHN 8:30-32

"You will know the truth, and the truth will set you free."
— John 8:32

DISCOVER

"It's just a little lie. It doesn't really matter." Have you ever found yourself saying words like that? If so, you've probably learned that trying to keep up with lies gets messy and complicated fast. It's easy to lie to keep up your reputation or to make a situation feel easier in the moment, but those things go away quickly. The hurt that comes from lying doesn't fade fast either.

If you've ever had a friend or family member lie to you, how hard was it to trust that person again? When you let truth invade every part of your life, there's freedom. There's nothing to hide, nothing to run from, and you're an open book. This sounds a lot easier than it is, but it should be your goal as you try to become more and more like Jesus.

Here's what's true about Jesus: He is truth. Everything about Him is right and good, and He can be trusted. Friend, the truth literally sets you free because Jesus is truth. When we spend time in the Bible and really get to know Him, truth is revealed to us through His words.

When we share about Jesus with others, we stand on a firm foundation of truth. As you center your life around Him, it takes the guesswork out of how you should live and what you should do, because you'll find yourself going back to the Bible to find truth. Knowing Jesus truly does change your life and set you free.

DELIGHT

How would you explain our key verse today to someone else?

Is truth important to you? Why or why not?

DISPLAY

If you've struggled with lying, breaking that habit may not come easily, but God's desire is for you to be a person of truth. If you're nervous about people finding out the truth, it's very likely that the truth will come much better from you than them finding out from someone else. Ask God to help you as you share truth into dark places and give that area of your life (big or small) over to Him. He wants you to be a truth teller, and today is the perfect day to start.

God, help my heart for You and my words match one another. Let my words show the truth and help me to feel the freedom that comes with being a truth teller. Thank You for always being truthful with me.

DAY 20

OPPOSITES DON'T ATTRACT

READ GALATIANS 5:16-18.

I say, then, walk by the Spirit and you will certainly not carry out the desire of the flesh.
— Galatians 5:16

DISCOVER

When we "walk by the Spirit" we are living like Jesus. After we choose to follow Jesus, God sends the Holy Spirit to be our guide. If you trust Jesus and you've ever thought that your conscience was guiding you, what was guiding you was actually the Holy Spirit. These verses today explain that the Spirit and the flesh (that is, our own desires) are constantly battling against one another. They are fighting for completely different things and giving glory to opposite places.

Think about it this way—if you're trying to decide whether or not to go to a party Saturday night, knowing you probably won't want to get up for church the next morning, your flesh and Spirit are fighting one another. You might say to yourself, "My flesh wants to go out with my friends, but the Spirit is reminding me the importance of being in church community." The Spirit guides you to do the right thing and helps you as you make decisions. God isn't like a puppet master in the sky who is making you do things. He has given you the choice to make decisions, face consequences, receive rewards, and to live out what you believe on a daily basis.

When your focus is on what God wants and how you can honor Him with every area of your life, the whole situation shifts. It's not about what you can and can't do anymore—everything begins to align with God's best, and that's where you make decisions from, not from your flesh. It's an amazing thing to experience, and it's what knowing God in a deeper way brings into your life. It's the place where you no longer desire what you want, but what He wants.

DELIGHT

Do you choose to live more in the flesh or the Spirit? Why?

How do you know if you're walking in the Spirit? How do you know if you're walking in the flesh?

DISPLAY

Pursuing Jesus with everything you have truly brings freedom. You are set free to walk in the Spirit and to do it with confidence and joy. Walking by the Spirit is where God does His best work in our lives because it's not about us. Let God have this and your life will change!

Pray that God would move you toward living in the Spirit instead of living in the flesh. Ask Him to give you boldness and courage to make tough choices and trust Him with the outcome.

SECTION 3

HOW TO USE OUR FREEDOM

As you live set free, Jesus is on display for everyone around you to see. You'll be willing to go wherever He calls you and do whatever you can for His name. You are never alone, and the example Jesus set for you will guide you!

DAY 21

ONE STEP BACK

READ GALATIANS 5:1-6.

For freedom, Christ set us free. Stand firm, then, and don't submit again to a yoke of slavery.
— Galatians 5:1

DISCOVER

Jesus gives us everything we need, but we often settle for less. He has already won the battle, while we're over here trying to fight off the enemy with a wet noodle because we think we have to do the work Jesus already accomplished. Jesus's righteousness is given to you, and you didn't have to work for it! He set us free from the law and from having to earn our salvation.

The world tells you to fill the void in your life with everything except for Jesus. It's crazy because none of that will ever make you happy or fill you up. It's like a bottomless pit—no matter how much you try to fill it up, it will never be full. You'll always be left wanting more. Phrases like "You only live once," "Live your best life," and "You are enough" are ways that the world tries to tell us that Jesus isn't enough. But He is more than enough!

Why is it that we find ourselves taking a step back and doing what we used to do before we knew Jesus? We go back to our old ways, old friends, and old sins, and then we end up in a mess. Those things are the "yoke of slavery" that today's key verse mentions. They're the things that used to have a hold on us before we were set free, yet we keep going back to them. Only when we experience and embrace true freedom through the Holy Spirit retraining our minds and hearts will we truly be set free!

DELIGHT

What's an area of your old life that you keep going back to? Why is it so hard to give up?

What is God asking you to do so that you can truly walk in freedom with Him?

Is living set free worth it? Why or why not?

DISPLAY

For Jesus to be enough, He has to have access to every area of our lives (in fact, He already does, but He wants for us to give it to Him). He's right there, waiting on us to come to Him, ready to walk in freedom. Friend, what's holding you back? Who is a trusted friend or mentor who loves Jesus and whom you can talk to about the things that are keeping you from fully walking with Jesus? Make some time as soon as you can to talk to him or her and be encouraged!

God, I want to live set free. Thank You for the gift of righteousness through Jesus. Help me to let go of the old things and run to You!

DAY 22

POWER PLAY

READ GALATIANS 5:13-15.

For you were called to be free, brothers and sisters;
only don't use this freedom as an opportunity for the flesh,
but serve one another through love.
— Galatians 5:13

DISCOVER

In these verses, Paul is writing to the churches in Galatia and reminding them that living set free isn't about having the ability to do whatever they want but about serving others well. Freedom and humility go hand in hand. Jesus didn't come to the earth to be served, but to serve others, no matter who He was with or where He was. Jesus knew His life wasn't about drawing attention to Himself—it was always about how He could glorify God in every situation. When we seek to serve and not be served, it takes the attention off of us and puts it in the right place.

We can't use the freedom we have in Christ as an opportunity to hold power over anyone else. Our freedom in Jesus gives us the opportunity and ability to serve in love. I often pray that God would help me see others the way that He sees them. I tend to look at other people through the lens of either what others say about them and their reputation or through their words and their actions. But God sees people differently. When I try to look at people through God's eyes, it changes my perspective and helps me to see how I can serve in a way that helps them and honors God.

DELIGHT

Have you ever thought you could do whatever you wanted because you knew God would forgive you? Does that line up with the Bible? Why or why not?

Who are your "neighbors"? How can you serve them?

DISPLAY

Why is it so easy for us to feel like we can do whatever we want to do? The world tells us that we are in charge of our own lives, but the Bible says the opposite. Think of some ways you can serve the people whom God puts in your path this week. Pray that He gives you a new, unique opportunity to show Him to the people in your circle.

Pray that God would give you the chance to serve this week. Ask Him to guide and direct you and for it to be completely about Him, not you. Surrender anything that may get in your way.

DAY 23

20/20

READ 2 CORINTHIANS 3:7-18.

For our momentary light affliction is producing for us an absolutely incomparable eternal weight of glory.
— 2 Corinthians 4:17

DISCOVER

It's amazing how many times we find the word *freedom* in the Bible. It's truly all over the place, especially in the New Testament. When something's repeated that much, we definitely need to pay attention.

If you read all of the verses for today, you'll see that there's a lot of talk about "veils." What Paul is getting at is that before Jesus, there was an old covenant that the people followed. There was a veil (like a thick curtain or a separation) between the people and God. Under the new covenant that Jesus brought, that veil is gone! We have total access to God because of Jesus. There's an amazing freedom that comes with the removal of this separation from God.

The Holy Spirit lives within us and is transforming us to be more like Jesus every day. That's true freedom right there. As we grow and mature in our faith, we find more and more freedom because we look more and more like Jesus. We aren't tied to the things of this world—only to Him. When we come to know Jesus and the veil is removed, it's like we finally have 20/20 vision! Jesus gives a clarity that we can't find any other way. There's freedom when we have sight: our trust is stronger and we know there's a light leading the way.

DELIGHT

What was your life before Jesus like? How would you describe it in a few words?

What can you see differently or with more clarity now that you know Him as your Lord and Savior?

How has living in freedom changed your life?

DISPLAY

If you've experienced freedom, you'll never want to be veiled again. Jesus truly does change your life! The freedom He offers is unique and is something we should talk about with everyone we encounter. Live in it, my friend! Think about one way you could share the freedom and joy you have found in Christ with someone today. Write about it below.

Pray that God would help you to live an unveiled life where you can walk fully in the freedom He has given you. Ask Him to help you when you feel stuck or need His guidance. He is there, waiting for you!

DAY 24

WHO'S THE BOSS?

READ 1 PETER 2:11-17.

Submit as free people, not using your freedom as a cover-up for evil, but as God's slaves.
— 1 Peter 2:16

DISCOVER

One of the hard things about walking in freedom is submitting to authorities you may not agree with. I'm guessing there's someone in authority over you who you don't completely agree with. It could be your parents, a teacher or coach, a government authority, or some other leader in your life. It would be easy to say you submit to God, not people, but Peter is saying you still need to respect human authorities, even if they aren't Christian. Your job is to honor God and leave the rest up to Him. The good works that you will do give glory to God and respect to those in authority. But let's be clear: Even though we are called to obey other people, when an authority in your life pushes you to disobey God, you should not follow those instructions.

When you do good and honor God, it matters. We should never use our freedom in Christ to do evil, but we should freely submit ourselves to Jesus and follow Him wherever He leads. He is worth it! It's never right to disobey God or His Word. Let those around you see that something is different in your life and that it's because of God. Let your actions and words point other people toward Him, even if you're alone in doing it.

Your freedom in Christ should always bring glory to Him. That's where things are so different from how the world would see freedom. It's not about you at all—it's all about God. You can rest easier, knowing that it doesn't all depend on you.

DELIGHT

Who is an authority in your life you struggle to submit to? Why is it difficult?

What does living in freedom look like in your life right now?

DISPLAY

Let your freedom be on display in a way that honors God and points to Him, not to you. Be willing and ready to follow His lead no matter what. He can always be trusted! He won't ever point you in the wrong direction. What is one way you can reveal your obedience to Him by submitting to the godly authorities in your life today?

God, give me rest in Your freedom. Show me how to give respect to the authorities in my life and point to You at the same time. Help me to be courageous in these situations.

DAY 25

SNACK ATTACK

READ 1 CORINTHIANS 6:12-20.

"Everything is permissible for me," but not everything is beneficial. "Everything is permissible for me," but I will not be mastered by anything.
— 1 Corinthians 6:12

DISCOVER

Obedience and freedom go hand in hand. Today's key verse is one that people often misquote or use out of context. There are a lot of things in the world that are permissible, but many of them have no good benefit. It's a waste of our time to do things that don't have any benefit to us or to God. God meant for us to enjoy life and the goodness that He created for us, but it needs to be enjoyed in a way that honors God and shows our obedience towards Him. We are free to use our bodies to glorify God, not misuse them for our own desires. Our job is to glorify God with our bodies, not gratify ourselves alone.

Our verses for today are talking about sexual immorality, but the same idea can be applied to so many situations. Think back to when you were a kid—what was your favorite sweet snack? Maybe it was ice cream (me!), candy, a donut, or something else amazing. Did your parents let you have that snack every day? My guess is they probably didn't, even though you may have wanted that sprinkle donut all the time. Your parents were looking out for your best—what was best for your body and what was best for your energy and health. God doesn't withhold good things from us—He just wants us to have and use them in the right way so that it honors us and Him.

DELIGHT

What are some areas of your life that may be permissible but are not beneficial?

Think about a couple of ways you can begin to change that area to make sure they honor God. List them below.

DISPLAY

Becoming set free and more like Jesus isn't an overnight change—it's a lifelong journey. We should try to make intentional changes on a regular basis to become more and more like Him. Some changes may require you to make tough decisions and change up some of the people in your life, but Jesus is worth it! Is there a habit or relationship that needs to change in your life today? What is one way you can bring that situation into submission to God?

God, show me ways I can honor You with my body today. If there are changes I need to make, help me to do it in a way that brings You glory and points other people toward You.

DAY 26

TWISTS AND TURNS

READ JAMES 1:22-25.

But the one who looks intently into the perfect law of freedom and perseveres in it, and is not a forgetful hearer but a doer who works—this person will be blessed in what he does.
— James 1:25

DISCOVER

Have you ever ridden a roller coaster? I absolutely love them. The thrill, the screaming, the unexpected twists and turns. To to ride one, you have to follow instructions, especially the one about buckling your seatbelt. Because once you get on the ride, there's no turning back. I vividly remember screaming all the way up a massive hill on my first roller coaster. I don't know how it would be humanly possible to ride a roller coaster and not react to what's going on around you.

In the same way, you can't just sit in a service at church and hear a sermon, sing along with the music, and talk about how great it was—and then not respond or do anything about it. What's the point in that? If you're just a consumer and not actually taking any of it and putting it into practice, you're wasting your time. We are meant to go, do, take action, and walk faithfully with Jesus. Our faith isn't a boring one—it's the best roller coaster you'll ever ride.

If you just listen to God's Word and think that's enough, you've missed the point. It's meant to transform us from the inside out and set us free. This is huge, so don't miss it! Going to church services, spending time reading the Bible, growing alongside other believers, and participating in other spiritual disciplines transforms us from the inside out. So hop on for the ride!

DELIGHT

When was the last time you can remember not just hearing something about God but actually doing something with what you heard? Write about it.

What has helped you grow as a Christian? List as many things as you can think of.

DISPLAY

God wants us to do something with what we know about Him. You could dream all day about being a marathon runner, but the first step is starting to run. Just thinking about running will literally get you nowhere fast. How can you take a step toward Jesus today and begin to put some things into practice and get your feet moving?

Ask God to show you how to not just be a hearer but also a doer. Tell Him why it's important to you and how much you love Him for who He is in your life.

MEMORY VERSE

FOR YOU WERE CALLED TO BE FREE, BROTHERS AND SISTERS; ONLY DON'T USE THIS FREEDOM AS AN OPPORTUNITY FOR THE FLESH, BUT SERVE ONE ANOTHER THROUGH LOVE.

GALATIANS 5:13

DAY 27

STUMBLING BLOCK

READ ROMANS 14:19-23.

So then, let us pursue what promotes peace and what builds up one another.
— Romans 14:19

DISCOVER

Is there anyone younger than you who looks up to you? It could be someone who plays the same sport or instrument you do, someone you've talked to in the lunchroom at school, or maybe even a younger sibling or cousin. Hopefully you want to set a good example for that person, so you wouldn't do something that would get her or him hurt or in trouble.

Have you heard someone say, "Don't be a stumbling block"? Part of your responsibility as a believer is to not cause others to sin. You're called instead to bring peace and help build others up. Your words and actions matter, and if people are following you, this is a massive reminder to make wise choices and set an example worth following. Whether it's the music you listen to, the people you follow, what you post on social media, or how you treat the people you're around, there's nothing you can hide from God, and there's very little you can hide from other people.

Don't do anything you wouldn't want someone else to also do. If this idea doesn't convict you, maybe it's time to refocus and think about whether you're really living set free in Jesus.

DELIGHT

Who's someone who looks up to you? How can you encourage this person and point her or him toward Jesus with your words and actions?

Have you ever set a bad example for others? Write out an example. How would you do things differently now?

DISPLAY

It's such a privilege to be able to set an example for others and not be a stumbling block. While you're never going to be perfect, you have a responsibility to let others see Jesus in you and do things that bring Him honor and glory. Even if you're only around strangers, you still have to live this out well, because God knows and sees it all! What is one thing you can do today to build someone up and be an encourager rather than a stumbling block?

look more and more like You every day. Don't
ling block; instead, help me be example whom
ecause I'm following You. Thank You for the
ccountable and to encourage others.

DAY 28

TELL HIM ABOUT IT

READ PSALM 118.

I called to the Lord in distress;
the Lord answered me
and put me in a spacious place.
— Psalm 118:5

DISCOVER

Does prayer ever seem difficult or intimidating to you? When it comes to talking to God, you truly can just talk to Him. You don't have to use fancy words. You can talk to him just like a friend. This psalm gives several great examples of things God does and who He is. In fact, the entire book of Psalms is a great tool for learning how to pray.

God always hears us! How incredible is it to know and believe that? Not only does He hear us, but He also answers us. It may not always be in the timing we want or the way we expected, and He doesn't always say yes to our requests, but He is good and faithful. The more time you spend in the Bible, the more you'll realize that this is a clear way God speaks to His people. He reminds us of what has happened in the past and what He has promised us for today.

Whether you're in a good situation or a hard one, God hears you. He sets you free to rest in Him and trust Him with whatever is going on in your life. You can call out to Him in prayer any time of the day or night and He hears you. There's nothing you can say that will scare Him away or make Him love you any less. Whatever is going on, tell Him and trust Him.

DELIGHT

Who is the first person you call when something big is going on in your life? Why is this person your first call?

Look back at Psalm 118. What are some of the things the writer says about who God is?

DISPLAY

Why is it so difficult to go to God sometimes even when we know what He can do? It's something that many people wrestle with, but God wants us to open the line of communication and talk to Him, no matter what's going on. He loves you and longs to set you free. What's holding you back? Spend a few minutes in prayer today. Don't rush it or force it. Just talk to God, and don't forget to listen as well.

God, thank You that You always hear me and care about me. Help me to run to You first and trust You with the way that You work in my life.

DAY 29

LEAST LIKELY

READ EPHESIANS 3:1-12.

In him we have boldness and confident access through faith in him.
— Ephesians 3:12

DISCOVER

Paul gives a really quick overview in these verses about how crazy it is that *he,* of all people, is the one writing about Jesus. He was once a persecutor of Christians and hated everything they stood for, until He met God in a very real way. After that, he did a complete 180 degree turn and started encouraging and helping Christians any way he could. Paul is an amazing example that God can use anyone for His glory, no matter that person's background.

Paul explains that the people reading his words are better able to understand the mystery of Christ because Jesus has already come. Jesus has finished His work on earth and has left His disciples and apostles to tell others what they know. Paul is making it clear that, in Jesus, we are free to be bold and confident in Him. Jesus has given us everything we need to do what He has called us to do.

We are set free to trust Jesus no matter the situation. If people reject us because of our faith, it's not us they're really rejecting, but Jesus. We should be willing to take the risk of rejection because our eternal reward is absolutely worth it. Paul was the least likely person to follow Jesus, but he became the person who was on fire for Jesus because his life had been so radically changed. It truly was a miracle!

DELIGHT

Who is someone you think might be too far away to ever know Jesus? Take some time and pray for him or her right now.

For the last few weeks, we've been talking about freedom in Christ. How would you explain freedom in Christ in your own words?

DISPLAY

Do you know a story of someone who met Jesus even though it was really unlikely? No matter your background, the fact that you know Jesus is just as amazing as it is for anyone else. Your story of knowing Him is unique and personal, so take every chance you have to share it with the people God puts in your life. Do it with boldness and confidence, knowing that Jesus is with you. Use the space below to write out your story of how you came to know Jesus.

God, thank You for the freedom You've given me to know You and walk with You, no matter where I was before I met You. You are so good and faithful. Thank You for seeing me right where I am and using me.

DAY 30

FULFILLED

READ LUKE 4:16-21.

"The Spirit of the Lord is on me, because he has anointed me to preach good news to the poor. He has sent me to proclaim release to the captives and recovery of sight to the blind, to set free the oppressed, to proclaim the year of the Lord's favor."
— Luke 4:18-19

DISCOVER

The speaker in today's verses is Jesus, and it's a total mic drop moment. Jesus had gone to His hometown of Nazareth, made His way to the synagogue, and sat down to read from the Old Testament (see Isa. 61:1-2). The verses He reads prophesy the coming Messiah, and after reading, He explains that this Scripture been fulfilled. He is the One the people have been waiting for. Boom.

In Jesus's day, the Jews were anticipating a Savior, but they expected that Savior to be an earthly king like David. Jesus wasn't that at all. So His own people rejected Him and had a hard time believing He could be the Messiah who fulfilled the Old Testament prophecies.

By reading these verses, Jesus is setting up everyone who comes after Him (including us) to carry out His ministry to serve others and spread the good news that everyone can be set free when they trust in Him. We have a big job to do, and it's to do everything we can to help others meet Jesus so they can also be set free. Are you up to the challenge?

Don't miss what Jesus has for you because you're worried about what others will think. Go back to the Bible and what it says so that you're reminded of the truth! Fulfill your calling and be confident in who Jesus made you to be. He's with you and He's in your corner. So follow Him!

DELIGHT

What can you do today to proclaim the good news of Jesus to the people around you?

In what areas of your life are you successfully living set free? In what areas do you still need some work?

DISPLAY

Jesus is worth the risk. He loves you so much and would do anything to show it to you. Your job is to trust Him with everything and to be bold in whatever He calls you to do. Make the most of any opportunity that God gives you, and remember: Jesus is with you, no matter what! He is always cheering you on and so are the other believers in your life. Keep your eyes fixed on Jesus, my friend!

God, give me what I need to be bold and courageous for You. I don't want to look anywhere but where You are, so help me stay focused and ready to do whatever You call me to do. You are good and I trust You!

FINDING TRUE FREEDOM

Imagine that you've just stepped out of a car with no AC, in the middle of summer, after an hours-long road trip. A breeze cools your skin the second you step outside. Maybe you stretch. Maybe you sigh in relief. Or maybe you stop to glimpse the amazing view of surrounding mountains, a glistening river, or the varied hues of a sunset. It can be tough to describe what we feel in moments like that, but some might say it's freedom.

Think about it: What is freedom to you? Highlight your answers from the options below.

To you, is freedom more like _____ or ________?

- Summer break ***or*** school-year routines?
- Following the rules ***or*** breaking some that seem harmless?
- Getting to choose where your family eats on Sunday after church ***or*** being allowed to have a friend over when your parents aren't home?
- Taking a vacation with your family ***or*** going to your favorite theme park with friends?
- Having your own car ***or*** getting your first job?
- Taking a gap year ***or*** starting college early?
- Speaking your mind ***or*** not having to say anything because the people around you just get you?

Now, write out your definition of freedom.

To many of us, freedom feels like permission to do whatever we want. It feels like the ability to make our own choices, especially when it comes to how we spend our time or who we spend it with. It feels like getting to say what we think, no matter what. Freedom often feels like having no rules, no boundaries, and no consequences.

But have you ever wondered why that kind of freedom feels a bit empty? Why it doesn't quite feel like freedom when you've done what you wanted to do and felt unsatisfied or when you've said whatever you wanted to and hurt someone?

The truth is, sometimes our feelings lie. They even lie to us about freedom.

All of us probably define freedom differently because we're unique people with varied stories and life experiences. But we know that God, the Author of our stories, is truth. So, if we want to know the true definition of freedom, we must look to Him.

True freedom, then, is not having permission to do whatever we want; it's knowing God and living out the fullness of His design for us.

Take a look at these two verses and in your own words write out what you think they mean:

2 Corinthians 3:17 –

Galatians 5:1 –

Much like stepping out of that hot car, freedom could be described as relief.

- Freedom is relief from believing that living the right way is all on you.
- Freedom is relief from not knowing who you are or what your purpose is.
- Freedom is relief that all the heavy things of life that you experience don't rest on your shoulders alone.
- Freedom is relief from the pressure of living up to (or down to) others' expectations of you.
- Freedom is relief from endless effort.

- Freedom is resting in Jesus: in the work He accomplished in His life, death, and resurrection; and in the hope of the future He has promised us—eternal life with Him.

Jesus's blood, poured out on the cross to cover our sin and our failure, frees those who trust in Him from the eternal consequences of their mistakes. But His gracious gift also frees us to certain things.

"If the Son sets you free, you really will be free." — John 8:36

Jesus frees us to:

- have a restored relationship with God;
- follow Him, even though we'll mess up;
- build healthier relationships with the people and creation around us;
- live in confidence, knowing our identity and future rest in Him, not in what we say or do or what others say or do; and
- enjoy eternal life with Him in the new heaven and earth.

Now, take a minute to think about what Jesus has freed you from specifically. Then consider what He has freed you to. Write out a prayer below, thanking Jesus for all that He has freed you from and all that He has freed you to do.